New Testament Bible Studies

■ ■ ■

Word for You

By Prince Handley

University of Excellence Press

Copyright © 2009 by Prince Handley
All Rights Reserved.

UNIVERSITY OF EXCELLENCE PRESS
Los Angeles ■ London ■ Tel Aviv

ISBN-13: 978-0692278864
ISBN-10: 0692278869

Printed in the U.S.A.

First Edition

Study and learn the WHOLE New Testament

TABLE OF CONTENTS

FOREWORD

WELCOME! You have just made a quality decision to improve your life NOW … and forever!

Many people have found eternal life and experienced MIRACLES--real miracles-- while doing these studies. **Questions are placed within the content**---not at the end of each chapter. **This makes it easy to learn**.

There are twelve (12) lessons: An introductory first lesson and ten others (Lesson Eight is divided into two parts). You will learn how to know Yeshua (Jesus), God's Son, in a personal way. You will learn how to walk with Him and how to please Him.

You will enjoy doing the lessons and learn at the same time. **All questions and study notes are placed within the text and direct the reader to the exact scripture**.

Do not skip the Introductory Lesson, *Joy is a Word*. Even though it is the easiest in the series, it is the one where you will make sure you know Messiah Jesus personally and are on your way to Heaven!

The lessons cover the whole New Testament of the Holy Bible and are designed to be studied in order, by their numbers. These Bible studies are different. They are designed to let you **know the core of the content** … and are **free from unnecessary minutiae**.

Some people like to study with a group---or alone---and then later, during the group session, compare answers for discussion.

When you finish the lessons, you will have a solid knowledge of the New Testament. Many people like to re-study the lessons once a year or periodically. Also, you can use the studies to teach others.

Bonus: An unabridged "Frequently Asked Questions" section to help you!

"You shall know the truth, and the truth shall make you free."

New Testament Bible Studies

■ ■ ■

Word for You

INTRODUCTORY LESSON

Joy is a Word!

In reading a book. it is always a good thing to know who wrote it. In 2 Peter 1:21 (that means the second book of Peter, chapter one, verse 21) the Holy Bible says, "For the telling of God's will (prophecy) did not come in ages past by man's own will: but holy men of God spoke as they were moved by the Holy Spirit." You can see from this that it was the Holy Spirit (the Spirit of God) who caused men to write the Holy Bible.

The Holy Bible also says in 2 Timothy 3:16, "All scripture (the Word of God) is given by inspiration of God ..." In other words, God inspired (or, gave life to) everything that is written in the Holy Bible. God used men to write down the words, but it was God himself who caused men to write the words as his Holy Spirit moved them!

The Holy Bible is the Word of God! Have you ever thought about what a "word" is? What does "word" mean. A "word" is a message. Or simply, it is a way to carry information. So the Word of God is God's message to man; it is God's way of reaching us.

In the Gospel of John, turn to Chapter One. Read the first verse.

Who was in the beginning?

_____

_____

_____

[Write your answers in the lines above.]

Where was the Word?

_____

_____

Who was the Word?

_____

_____

Now read verse 14 of John Chapter One. What was made flesh?

_____

_____

Jesus is the LIVING Word. He was God in human flesh. The Holy Bible is the WRITTEN Word. It tells us of God's love for us, and how he sent Jesus to die for our sins ... and how God raised him from the dead. Jesus is alive! Read verse 12 of Chapter One in the Gospel of John.

What happens to everyone who receives Jesus?

_____

_____

Have you ever received Jesus?

YES [ ]   NO [ ]

[Place an "X" in the right answer above]

Were you old enough to know what you were doing?

YES [ ]   NO [ ]

If you were to die right now, do you KNOW FOR SURE that you would go to Heaven?

YES [ ]   NO [ ]

The Holy Bible says, *"These things have I written to you ... that you may KNOW that you have eternal life."* [1 John 5:13]

Right now, if you have never received Jesus Christ into your life, or if you are not SURE that you have eternal life, you may invite Christ into your life. Simply pray this little prayer and mean it in your heart.

"Lord Jesus, I receive you into my life right now. I believe that you died on the cross for my sins, and I know that you are alive. Please forgive all of my sins; without you, I am lost. Please save me! In your name I pray."

_____

[Sign your name above]

Did you mean business? Were you sincere? Christ meant business on the cross ... when he took your place. He paid with his own blood a debt he did NOT owe (your sin debt), because you had a debt you could not pay. He took your place on the cross. Your sins were laid upon him. He was punished so that you could live forever.

Now turn to John 3:36. (Chapter 3, verse 36.) According to the Word of God, what would happen if you were to die right now? Would you experience:

Everlasting life? [ ] --**OR**-- God's judgment? [ ]
[Place an "X" in the right answer above]

If you have received Messiah (Christ), you are saved and have everlasting life. **Do NOT trust your feelings: your feelings change. Believe God's Word."** *Your Word is truth."* [John 17:17] If you know that you have everlasting life, you will begin to experience JOY in your life. To keep this joy, and to have VICTORY daily, practice these things every day:

> **Read the Word of God** (This way, God talks to you. Start and end your day with Bible reading.)

> **Pray** (You talk to God.)

> **Witness** (You tell others how you found Jesus, and how they may know him.)

Look at John 10:10. Jesus said, *"I have come that they might have life, and that they might have it more abundantly."* Now that you know Jesus (He is the source of life), you will want to know his Word (the Holy Bible) so you can have life **MORE ABUNDANTLY!** In John 8:31, Jesus said, *"If you continue in my word, then you are my disciples indeed."*

QUESTIONS

Who wrote the Bible?

_____

_____

How did God live (dwell) among men? (John 1:14)

_____

_____

What did Jesus say you must do to see the kingdom of God?

_____

_____

What is the "bread of God"? (John 6:28-35)

_____

_____

What is the "living water"? (John 7:38-39)

_____

_____

Your next study (Lesson 1) will be: *How to Have Fun in the Bible*. There are 12 lessons in this course. You will have studied the whole New Testament when you finish this course.

LESSON ONE

How to have fun in the Bible!

Would you like to have fun that never gets old? Wouldn't it be fun to be free from things which tie you down? How would you enjoy doing just what God wants you to do?!

The Holy Bible says, *"If the Son (Jesus, the LIVING Word) makes you free, then you will be really free."* (See the gospel of John you studied with your last lesson - John 8:36.)

How does Jesus set us free? Remember what we studied last time? When we read the WRITTEN Word, the Holy Bible, we find out how Jesus Christ died for our sins on the cross, was buried, and is alive again!

In this lesson we will study six books which are found in the New Testament (promise) of God's Word, the Holy Bible. The six books are as follows:

Galatians	Colossians
Ephesians	1 Thessalonians
Philippians	2 Thessalonians

Now what are all these funny names? They are the names of cities and states or provinces: just like Los Angeles, Nairobi, Paris, Tehran, Singapore, or Mexico City. God, by his Holy Spirit, caused a preacher named Paul to write to churches in other places.

The Apostle Paul was a Hebrew from the tribe of Benjamin who studied under Gamaliel, a member of the Jewish Sanhedrin (or, governing body of the Jews) and who was a well known Jewish rabbi of the day.

Paul wrote to a group of Messianic Synagogues (churches) in a place called Galatia to remind them that they are free. In Galatians 1:4, God tells us that we are set free from this present evil age because Messiah (Christ) willingly gave (or, sacrificed) himself for our sins. Read Galatians 2:21 through 3:3. How is man put right with God?

by God's Law [   ] --**OR**-- by Christ's death [   ]
[Place an "X" in the right answer.]

Freedom is what we have! Christ has set us free! (See Galatians 5:1.) If we are FREE - that is, joined to Christ, and not to the world - what is the only thing we can boast about? [Read Galatians 6:14.]

_____

_____
[Fill in the answer above]

The more we read God's Word, the more we see how much we have to be thankful for. In the book of Ephesians God shows us that in a special way the Jews are God's "chosen" people (Ephesians 2:12). But in another way, God has chosen all people who are joined to Christ to be his. When did God choose us? [See Ephesians 1:4.]

_____

_____

People who are not Jewish are called "Gentiles" (Gentiles are also referred to as "goyim.") Read carefully verses 13 through 18 in Chapter Two of Ephesians. How is it that all of us, both Jews and non-Jews (Gentiles), have access by the Holy Spirit to the Father God? How are we able to present ourselves by the Holy Spirit to God the Father?

_____

_____

In the book of Philippians, God shows us that he has a PLAN ... for our lives, and for the whole world. How long will God work in YOU, so that you may obey his plan? [See Philippians 1:6 and 2:13.]

_____

_____

What will all men do some day? [Ph. 2:10-11.]

_____

_____

The book of Colossians was written to remind people that they were dead in sin apart from Christ, but now they have TRUE LIFE if they are joined to Christ!

What four things should we do in being joined (that is, in union) with Christ? [See Colossians 2:6-7 . . . there are four (4) answers; use one line for each answer.]

_____

_____

_____

_____

Paul also tells us how we are to talk. How should you talk to God? [See Colossians 4:2 . . . there are three (3) answers; use one line for each answer.]

_____

_____

_____

How should you talk to people? [Colossians 4:5-6 . . . there are four (4) answers; use one line for each answer.]

_____

_____

_____

_____

In the books of 1st and 2nd Thessalonians, the preacher Paul reminds us of how we are to live in these last days, as well as telling us the world news ahead of time. When you watch TV or Internet News, or listen to the radio, you only know what has taken place in the PAST, or what is taking place NOW. However, the Holy Bible shows us the news ahead of time ... in the FUTURE!

Read carefully 1 Thessalonians 4:13-18. When the Lord Jesus comes back, who will go to meet him in the air first?

Dead Christians [ ]   --OR-- Living Christians [   ]
[Place "X" in the right answer]

Remember what Jesus said in John 11:25? "I am the resurrection and the life. Whoever believes in me will live, even though he dies ..." We should thank God at all times for our Christian brothers; God called us, with them, through the Good News (the Gospel). This is how e have FUN in the Holy Bible. Every day we can learn more about God, and how he set us FREE, so that we can enjoy life here on earth, and go to Heaven, too!

QUESTIONS

Are we saved by our good works? [Ephesians 2:8-9.]

YES [ ]   NO [ ]
[Place an "X" in the right answer above]

When Jesus returns, what happens to all who do not believe the truth, but take pleasure in sin? [2 Thessalonians 2:9-12.]

_____

Read Colossians 3:1-4. Where is your life?

_____

Your next study (Lesson 2) will be: **How to Talk to God.**

How to talk to God!

Think of the most important person you know! is it the leader of your nation ... or maybe someone who is a great preacher? Have you ever talked with them? Were you able to tell them everything you wanted to?

Really, who is the most important person in the world? Sure ... God! And if we have been born into God's family through faith in Jesus, we KNOW him ... he is our Father!

The wonderful thing about knowing God is that we can tell him everything we want to. Why? Because he is always with us. As a matter of fact, he wants us to talk to him. The Holy Bible says to "pray at all times." Pray means talk to God!

You see, prayer means more than just asking God for things. It is just like talking to anyone else. Use the simple little four letter guide spelled T-A-L-K to help you when you pray:

> **T** - Thank God.
> **A** - Adore (love) God.
> **L** - Level with God.
> **K** - Know that God hears when you ask!

T - **Thank God**. Thank him for everything he has given you - most of all, for Jesus! Thank him for even little things like your toothbrush. Thank God for even the hard times you have had, because he has taught you in them.

"Be thankful in all circumstances. This is what God wants of you, in your life in Christ Jesus." [1 Thessalonians 5:18.]

A - **Adore God**. Tell him how much you love him.

"This is how God showed his love for us: he sent his only Son into the world that we might have life through him." [1 John 4:9.]

L - **Level with God**. Confess your sins. Get everything out in the open.

"But if we confess our sins to God, we can trust him, for he does what is right - he will forgive us our sins and make us clean from all our wrongdoing." [1 John 1:9.]

K - **Know that God hears when you ask!** Ask for yourself ... and for others; ask firmly, but do NOT doubt in your heart.

"If you have faith, and doubt not ... you shall say ... and it shall be done." [Matthew 21:21.]

Have you ever prayed for something and you did not receive it right away? Read Luke 11:5-13. In verse 8, why did Jesus say the man's friend would give him everything he needed?

_____

_____

What will happen if you ask? [Verse 9.]

_____

_____

What will happen if you knock? [Verse 9.]

_____

_____

Did you ever go to a friend's house and knock on the front door, but no one came to the door, and so you went to the side or back door and knocked until someone answered? Remember, when you call on God, he is always there!

Jesus said, *"There are many rooms in my Father's house ..."* [John 14:2.] Just as there are many rooms in God's house, there are many doors to knock at when praying. If you don't get the answer at the front door, try the side door!

Note: the books of 1, 2, and 3 John are different than the Gospel of John.

Below are listed six doors you may knock at when you ask God for things:

Door 1 - **Do God's will** [1 John 3:22; John 15:16]

"We receive from him whatever we ask, because we obey his commands and do what pleases him."

Door 2 - **Pray in Jesus' name** [John 14:14]

"If you ask me for anything in my name, I will do it."

Door 3 - **Ask in faith** [Matthew 21:22.]

"If you believe, you will receive whatever you ask for in prayer."

Door 4 - **Agree with someone** [Matthew 18:19.]

" ... whenever two of you on earth agree about anything you pray for, it will be done for you by my Father in Heaven."

Door 5 - **Believe you have it already** [Mark 11:24.]

"When you pray and ask for something, believe that you have received it, and everything will be given you."

Door 6 - **Keep praying** [Luke 11:5-13]

" ... and give you everything you need because you are not ashamed to keep on asking ... knock, and the door will be opened to you."

Sometimes our prayers are not answered because of bad reasons for asking, or because we are not living like God wants us to!

QUESTIONS

How did Jesus like to pray most of the time? [Luke 9:18.]

_____

How long did Jesus pray before choosing his 12 disciples? [Luke 6:12.]

_____

Which part of **T-A-L-K** did Jesus use in his prayer in Luke 10:21?

_____

Read Luke 22:39-46. What did Jesus warn his disciples to pray about?

_____

EXTRA

Read Luke 18:10-14. The Pharisee thanked God (**T**) but he did not level (**L**) with him. The tax collector, however, leveled with God – he confessed his sin!

Your next study (Lesson 3) will be: *How to Follow Christ.*

How to follow Messiah (Christ)!

Have you ever tried to be like someone else? Maybe you've tried to talk like them, or to act like them, or maybe you have just dressed like them. Really, you could never be like them, could you? Why? Because you are yourself, that's right - you're YOU!

You know, when you decided to follow Christ, you died. Not only did you die, but you became a new person - IN CHRIST! The Holy Bible says, *"When anyone is joined to Christ he is a new being; the old is gone, the new has come."* [2 Corinthians 5:17.]

▩ NOTE ▩

The name "Christ" comes from the word "Messiah" which means "anointed" or "Anointed One." The Messiah (Hebrew, **Mashiach**) is the Promised One, the deliverer promised by the God of Israel for the salvation of all people, and the King who will deliver the Jewish People in the last days and set up His Kingdom in Israel, ruling from Jerusalem.

Since you are a new person and want to follow Jesus the Messiah, you will want to find how God wants you to live. God used the preacher Paul (Rabbi Shaul) to write some letters to three men named Timothy, Titus, and Philemon to tell them how God wanted them to live.

These letters are included in the New Testament of the Holy Bible. (A testament is a "will, a covenant, a contract, or a promise.) Also, a letter to the Hebrews (no one knows who the Holy Spirit used to write to the Hebrews). When you read these books (letters), you will learn more about how God wants you to live, so that you can follow Christ.

▩ NOTE ▩
In Hebrew the New Testament is called
"Brit Chadashah" for New Covenant.

Paul wrote two letters to a young man he had led to Christ named Timothy. The first letter tells how to live in order to have a clear conscience before God and man. Paul told Timothy not to let anyone look down upon him because he was young. In what ways did Paul tell him to be an example? [See 1 Timothy 4:12.]

_____

Verse 14 of Chapter Four shows that Timothy had a spiritual gift. How was it imparted (or, given) to him?

_____

_____

_____

Read 1 Timothy 6:6-10. The Holy Bible shows us the danger of wanting riches. Now read verse 11. What should you strive for?

_____

In the second book (or, letter) to Timothy, the Holy Spirit used Paul to show us the importance of training and teaching. That is, how we should train to serve God, and then teach others what we have learned. We should "stir up," or keep alive the gifts we receive from God and the things we learn, and then we should teach others to do the same. [See 2 Timothy 1:6.]

In 2 Timothy 1:7, the Holy Bible tells us that the Holy Spirit which God gives us does not make us timid - we do NOT have a spirit of fear; but God's Spirit fills us with three (3) things. What are they?

_____

_____

Therefore, we should not be ashamed to witness for our Lord! [See verse 8.]

The Holy Bible tells us to take part in suffering for the Good News as a loyal soldier of Christ Jesus. [2 Ti 2:3-7.] Not only does God tell us to be like a soldier, but also like an athlete and a farmer. In your own words, tell how we should be like:

☞ A Soldier

_____

_____

☞ A Farmer

_____

_____

☞ An Athlete

_____

_____

God also tells us how to be used for SPECIAL purposes. Read carefully 2 Timothy 2:20-21. What can we do if we want to be used for special purposes? [See verse 21 and 22.]

_____

The Holy Spirit used Paul to write a young man named Titus to remind him that God wants us to live a "pure" life. He taught Titus how we should treat others, and how we should act toward those who are in charge of us.

_____

Read Titus 1:15-16. Why is nothing pure to some people?

_____

_____

Chapter Two of Titus tells us how older men and women, younger people, and workers should live and treat each other [verses 1-10]. Why should we use sound words that cannot be criticized when we talk to others? [See verse 8.]

_____

_____

Read Titus 3:1-2. How should we act toward rulers and authorities?

_____

_____

The book of Philemon is short but very important. Paul had led a young man to Christ named Onesimus, who was a run-away slave. Paul had urged him to return to his master, Philemon. This letter was written to Philemon, asking him to take Onesimus back and to forgive him.

Where was Paul when he became Onesimus' "spiritual father" (that is, when he led him to Christ)? [See verse 10.]

_____

The book of Hebrews is a tremendous book! It explains to us how the animals the children of Israel used to kill for a blood sacrifice for sins were really pictures (types) of the Lord Jesus Christ. Every time the priest would kill a lamb and pour its blood upon the altar, it was just a picture of how Jesus would come to earth as the LAMB of God to shed his blood on the cross for our sins!

After Jesus shed his blood on the cross for our sins, the priests of Israel did not need to pour out the blood of animals any longer. The blood which Jesus shed on the cross was the one FINAL complete payment for sin which pleased God!

Read Hebrews 9:14. What will the shed blood of Messiah (Christ) do for our consciences?

_____

_____

How long is Yeshua (Jesus) able to save those who come to God through him? [Hebrews 7:25.]

_____

Why?

_____

_____

▦ **NOTE** ▦

"Yeshua" is the original Hebrew name for "Jesus."

Is there another chance for salvation after this life on earth? [Hebrews 9:27.]

YES [ ]   NO [ ]
[Place an "X" in the right answer above]

Now that you are a NEW person, you will want to have God's POWER in your life. You will learn how in the next lesson. Your next study (Lesson 4) will be: *How to Receive the Power of God!*

How to receive
the power of God!

Isn't it wonderful to be a new person? A few years ago you probably never dreamed how God would change your life. Isn't God good?!

The wonderful thing about knowing Jesus is that life gets fuller every day--if you let it! When Christ died on the cross for your sins, his blood not only paid for your sins, but it bought your freedom. Jesus wants you to share this GOOD NEWS with others--to tell them he's alive.

Shortly before Jesus went back to Heaven, he said," ... that in his name the message about repentance and the forgiveness of sins must be preached to all nations ..." [Luke 24:47.]

Jesus did not ask you to do this job alone. He promised to send you a "gift" of POWER which would help you. Jesus said that he would send this promise upon you himself. "And I myself will send upon you what my Father has promised." [Luke 24:49.]

The book of Acts you will study in this lesson will tell you how to receive this "gift" (the promise of the Father). The Holy Spirit used a man named Luke, who was a follower of Jesus, to write both the book of Acts and the book of Luke. (Luke is the gospel which you studied with Lesson Two.)

In the book of Luke, Luke tells us how Jesus did his miracles by the POWER of the Holy Spirit - in the book of Acts, Luke tells us how the early followers of Jesus did their miracles by the POWER of the Holy Spirit. You, also - as a follower of Jesus - are to do the same kind of miracles by the POWER of the Holy Spirit!

As a matter of fact, Jesus said, "Whoever believes in me will do the works I do - yes, he will do even greater ones, for I am going to the Father." [John 14:12.] You see, the promise of the Father, the "gift" which Jesus said he, himself, would send upon his followers after he would go back to Heaven, was made to YOU, also!

"For God's promise was made to you and your children, and TO ALL who are far away - ALL whom he Lord our God calls to himself." [Acts 2:39.]

The last chapter in the Book of Luke and the first chapter in the book of Acts overlap. That is, they partly cover the same events. Read Acts Chapter One, verses 1-5. Jesus told his followers that God the Father had promised them a "gift." What was it? [See verse 5.]

_____

_____

The Holy Spirit lives in all those who follow Jesus - but to be baptized with the Holy Spirit is an extra gift. In John 20:22 (after Christ died on the cross and arose from the grave - before he went back to Heaven), Jesus breathed on his followers and said, "Receive the Holy Spirit." After this, the Holy Spirit was IN THEM, but as yet they had not been "baptized" with the Spirit.

To be "baptized" means to be overwhelmed or covered with. This is why Jesus told his followers (even though the Holy Spirit was already IN THEM), " ... wait in the city until the POWER from above comes down upon you." [Luke 24:49.]

Read Acts 1:8. What did Jesus say his followers would be filled with when the Holy Spirit came upon them?

_____

He said they would be _____ for Him. < *Write in the answer.*

Acts 2:1-4 tells what happened as the followers of Jesus waited in the city of Jerusalem. What was the result of their being "filled" with the Spirit? [See verse 4.]

_____

Who did Peter say "poured out" the Holy Spirit on the followers of Jesus? [Acts 2:32-33.]

_____

Bonus Question: What are four (4) different references (Bible Verses) that prove Jesus is **"The Baptizer"** in the Holy Spirit? [The answer is in each of the four Gospels: Matthew, Mark, Luke, and John.]

_____

_____

The Holy Spirit is the "gift" of POWER which God promised!

Study the following verses: Acts 10:44-48 and Acts 19:1-6. Remember in Acts 2:4 when the followers of Jesus were filled with the Holy Spirit--how they began to talk in other languages (strange sounds to the ones who were speaking)?

Read the following verses again and tell what they have in common with Acts 2:4

Acts 10:46 _____

_____

Acts 19:1-6 _____

_____

Remember the preacher Paul who we have studied about in other lessons? Before he was saved, his name was Saul (Rabbi Shaul). Just after he was saved, God sent a man named Ananias to pray for him. Read Acts 9:17-18. When Ananias laid hands upon Saul, what did he pray for?

_____

_____

In the book of 1 Corinthians, Paul said, "*I thank God that I speak with strange sounds (other tongues) much more than any of you.*" [1 Corinthians 14:18.] This was after Paul was filled with the Holy Spirit. What one thing seemed to happen each time you read about the Spirit coming down upon people?

_____

Study Acts 8:14-21 carefully. What do you suppose Simon saw that made him know that the Spirit had been given to them when the apostles laid their hands upon them? [See verse 18.]

_____

_____

Have you ever been "baptized" with the Holy Spirit? **If not, ask the Lord Jesus to baptize you right now**. Pray and wait on God until you receive this POWER! Tell the Lord how much you love him. Praise him! While you are praising him, simply shut off your own language (English or whatever language you speak), and start praising him in a NEW language the Holy Spirit will give you!

You will not understand your new language (neither will anyone else, unless it happens to be a language they know), but don't let that bother you. The Holy Bible says, *"The person who speaks with strange sounds (other tongues) does not speak to men but to God, because no one understands him. He is speaking secret truths by the power of the Spirit."* [1 Co. 14:2.]

Pray to God much in your new language. It will build you up, and then you will be able to build others up. 1 Corinthians 14:4 says, *"The man who speaks with strange sounds edifies (or, builds up) himself ..."*

Your next study (Lesson 5) will be: *How to Read God's Map.*

How to read God's map!

Mark's gospel is really a "map" in story form. It tells us about the "Lord's road" - the highway, or path, that Jesus traveled to the cross, where he died for our sins.

God sent a messenger named John ahead of the Lord Jesus to open the road, or way, for him. Read Mark 1:1-5. Why was he known as John the Baptist?

_____

_____

John told the people about the man who would come after him, the one whose way he was preparing. What did John the Baptist (not John, who wrote the gospel of John) say the man who would come after him would do? [See verse 8.]

_____

_____

Read Mark 1:9-11. What happened when John baptized Jesus in the Jordan River? [See verse 10.]

_____

_____

After Jesus was baptized in water and the Holy Spirit came down upon him, he began his ministry. He preached and told the people:

"Turn away from your _____ and believe the _____ _____." [Verse 15"]

What did Jesus tell Simon and Andrew they would catch if they came after him? [Mark 1:16-18.]

Read verses 21-28. How did Jesus teach? [Verse 22.]

_____

When Jesus commanded the unclean spirit out of the man in the synagogue, what happened? [See verse 26.]

_____

_____

The people said, **"This man has AUTHORITY!"**

Read Mark 1:32-34. What kind of diseases did Jesus heal? _____
[Write in your answer above.]

In verse 35, when did Jesus pray?

_____

Where?

_____

In Mark 1:40-45, a leper came to Jesus for help. When Jesus touched the leper and said, _"Be clean!,"_ how long did it take the leprosy to leave the man?

_____

Jesus came back to his home town after a few days and crowds gathered. Why did some teachers of the Law get upset when Jesus told a man, _"My son, your sins are forgiven?"_ [See Mark 2:7.]

_____

_____

28

How did Jesus prove to them that he had authority on earth to forgive sins? [Read verses 8-12.]

_____

_____

Jesus passed by a man who was collecting taxes. Jesus said, _"Follow me."_ What did the man do? [See verses 13-14.]

_____

Jesus went home to eat with him [Mark 2:15-17.] Some teachers of the Law who were Pharisees (a very strict religious sect) were disturbed because Jesus ate with outcasts (sinners) and tax collectors. Read what Jesus told them in verse 17. Who did Jesus say that he came to call?

_____

On another occasion, some of the religious people were mad because the disciples (followers and learners) of Jesus were picking grains of wheat to eat as they walked in the fields on the Sabbath (Holy Day of rest). They said, _"Look, it is against our Law for your disciples to do this on the Sabbath!"_ How did Jesus answer? [See verse 27.]

_____

_____

On the same day, Jesus went back to the synagogue, where there was a man who had a crippled hand. Why were some people watching Jesus very closely? [Mark 3:2.]

_____

Read Mark 3:3-6. Jesus asked the people: _"What does our Law allow us to do on the Sabbath? To help, or to harm? To save a man's life, or to destroy it?"_ Why did Jesus feel sorry for them, even though he was angry at them? [Verse 5.]

Jesus healed the man's hand, and after that the religious leaders left to meet with some members of Herod's party (the Roman government). Why? [Verse 6.]

_____

Later on, Jesus picked 12 men who he named as apostles (sent ones). Even though he would preach and teach to many large crowds, he chose these 12 men to stay with him so that he could teach them to do the same thing he was doing.

In Mark 3:13-15, Jesus was preparing them to send them out to:

_____

_____

_____

▓ NOTE ▓

There are 3 answers to the above question.
Memorize them because you are to do the same thing.

Some of the religious leaders accused Jesus of having the devil (Beelzebub) in him. They said that this was how he had the power to drive the demons out. Look how Jesus answered this in verses 23-30. What did Jesus say about the person who says evil things against the Holy Spirit?

_____

Read Mark 3:31-35. Who did Jesus say are his mother and brothers?

_____

_____

Study very carefully Mark 4:2-9. Now study carefully Jesus' explanation of this parable (teaching) in Mark 4:13-20. In your own words, tell how Jesus explained what the four soils were like.

☞ Path

_____

_____

_____

☞ Rocky ground

_____

_____

_____

☞ Thorns

_____

_____

_____

☞ Good soil

_____

_____

_____

We are to be "good soil." Jesus said, "You did not choose me; I chose you, and appointed you to go and bear much fruit, the kind of fruit that endures ..." [John 15:16.]

The rest of Mark's map tells us how Jesus continued his ministry of forgiving sins, healing the sick, and casting out demons. Jesus told his 12 followers several times how that he must go to the city of Jerusalem, and suffer many things, and be delivered up to die. But he also told them how he would rise again from the dead on the third day!

After Jesus was raised from the dead, he again appeared to his disciples. (Read Mark 16:14-26.) He told them to preach the "Good News" to all people!

Your next study (Lesson 6) will be: *How to Walk in the Light.*

How to walk in the light!

The Holy Bible is a book of light. Jesus is the light of the world. We are to be lights in the Lord, so that we will shine in the world. There are seven books in the Bible that are written to us as followers of Messiah Jesus to tell us how to shine for Jesus; they are:

- James

- 1 and 2 Peter

- 1, 2 and 3 John

- Jude

The book of James was written to show how our faith causes action (works) and how we can have victory in trials and temptations. James tells us how we should consider ourselves fortunate when all kinds of trials come our way. Why? [See James 1:2-4.]

_____

_____

What can we do if we ever need wisdom in any situation? [See James 1:5.]

_____

Read James 1:12-15. When is a person tempted? [Verse 14.]

_____

_____

_____

What is the final result? [Verse 15.]

_____

The Holy Bible, in James 1:26, says a man's religion is worthless if he does not:

_____

How can you make the devil flee from you? [See James 4:7.]

_____

_____

■ THE WORD OF GOD IS YOUR WEAPON ■
USE THIS VERSE IN JAMES 4:7 AGAINST SATAN
AND WATCH THE DEVIL RUN!

Study James5:14-15. What should you do when you are sick? [Verse 14.]

_____

_____

_____

What will be the result? [Verse 15.]

_____

_____

_____

The book of 1 Peter explains to us the purpose of trials and the reason for living holy. Read 1 Peter 1:6-7. What is the purpose of trials?

Why must we live holy? [1 Peter 1:15-16.]

_____

What was Noah's flood a figure (picture) of? [Look at 1 Peter 3:18-22.]

_____

Water baptism is only for those who are saved; those who have of their own will received the Lord Jesus and been born again. Have you been baptized in water since you believed?   Yes [   ]   No [   ] < Check one of the boxes to answer.

_____

Why should we be happy if we are insulted for following Christ? [Read 1 Peter 4:12-16.]

_____

_____

_____

What should you do with your worries? [1 Peter 5:7.] Also, explain "Why?"

_____

_____

_____

The book of 2 Peter tells us how that false teachers will appear in the last days and how this world will end. In 2 Peter 1:3-9 we read of eight qualities we need in order to be active and effective for the Lord. Why does Peter tell us to try harder in verse 10?

_____

Chapter 2 warns us that false teachers shall appear among us - it tells us how they will act and what they will say. Who will they deny? [Verse 1.]

_____

_____

_____

God tells us in Chapter 3:1-8 that in the last days there will be people whose lives are to be controlled by their own passions. What will they say and do to you? [Verse 3.]

_____

_____

Why is God patient with the world? [See verse 9.]

_____

_____

Verse 10 tells us that the Day of the Lord will come as a: _____.
                                        [Write in your answer.]

What will happen on that day?

_____

_____

_____

The books of 1, 2, and 3 John show us not only how to live in the light, but how to love. Study 1 John 1:5-10. God is light and there is no darkness at all in him. If we live in the light, what two things result? [See verse 7.]

_____

_____

If we say that we have no sin, what do we do to ourselves? [1 John 1:8.]

_____

_____

_____

What will happen if we confess our sins? [See verse 9.]

_____

_____

How can we check to see if the love of the Father is in us? [1 John 2:15-16.]

_____

_____

_____

Why doesn't the world know us now that we are in Christ? [1 John 3:1.]

_____

_____

What happens if our heart condemns us?[1 John 3:19-20.]

_____

_____

Study 1 John 4:4-6. In your own words describe how we can tell the difference between **the Spirit of Truth** and **the spirit of error**.

_____

_____

What should you do if anyone comes to you who does not bring the teaching of the Holy Bible? [2 John, verses 10, 11.]

_____

_____

The book of Jude tells us how to fight on for the complete faith which God gives us. How does Jude say to keep building yourself up, in your most sacred faith? [Verses 20, 21.]

_____

_____

You have five more lessons, and you will have completed the whole New Testament. The rest of the lessons are especially important: you will begin to know what's happening today ... and the news in advance!

Your next study (Lesson 7) will be: *How to Learn God's Program.*

How to learn God's program

Have you ever wondered if God has a **master plan**? You know, like a plan of the ages, or a program for the world? Well, he does! And it is all written in the Holy Bible for you to learn.

In the book of Romans you will learn about sin – where it came from and how God made a way to set us free. You will learn about God's Law – why it was given and how it had no strength to change our human nature. You will also learn about the nation Israel – what God has planed for her.

The Holy Spirit used the apostle Paul to write the followers of Jesus in Rome to tell them about salvation and their new life, as well as God's program for the world. When was the Good News first promised? [Romans 1:2]

_____

_____

The gospel (Good News) is God's power, or God's dynamite! What will it do? [Romans 1:16]

_____

_____

Why does God punish men who sin? [Romans 1:19]

_____

How will God reward every person? [Romans 2:6]

_____

God gave the Law of Moses to the Jews (the people of Israel) so that they would know when they sinned. (Read Romans 3:19-20.) The Law is like a mirror. When we look into it, we see our imperfections (sin).

_____

_____

_____

Why are both Jews and non-Jews (Gentiles) judged under sin? [Romans 2:12-16]

_____

_____

_____

How does God put men right? [Romans 3:22]

_____

Who needs to be saved? [Romans 3:23]

_____

How did God show us how much he loves us? [Romans 5:8]

_____

_____

Read Romans 5:12. When Adam (the first man who ever lived) sinned, what happened to the human race?

_____

_____

Just as sin ruled by means of death, how does God's grace rule those who receive it? [Romans 5:21]

_____

_____

How should we give ourselves to God? [Romans 6:13]

_____

_____

_____

How have we been set free from the law of sin and death? [[Romans 8:2]

_____

_____

**There is NO condemnation now for those
who live in union with Christ Jesus!**

Study Romans 8:8-14 carefully. What happens if we obey our human nature?

_____

What happens if we obey God's Spirit?

_____

_____

_____

How do we know that we are God's children? [See Romans 8:16]

_____

_____

No matter what happens to you, if you love God and are called according to his purpose, God works [_____] things for good. [Romans 8:28]

Write your answer in the box [_____] above.

IF GOD BE FOR US, WHO CAN BE AGAINST US? [Romans 8:31]

The apostle Paul was Jewish. (His Jewish name was Shaul, or Saul.) Read what sorrow he had in his heart for his own people. [Romans 9:2] He wanted them to know their Messiah (the Christ ... the Anointed One) personally, as he did. For centuries the Jews had waited for the Messiah. The prophets in the Tanakh (the Jewish Scriptures, or Old Testament) had written of him, how that he would come and be their king, the Holy One of Israel.

Yet they did not realize that first he must come as the lamb of God to die for our sins, before he would come back as King: the Lion of the tribe of Judah. John said, "He came unto his own (Israel, the Jews) and his own received him not. But as many as received him, to them gave he power to become the sons of God ..." [John 1:11-12]

Did God reject his own people (the Jews)? [See Romans 11:1-6]

When the nation of Israel did not receive Yeshua (Jesus) at his first coming, salvation came to the goyim (Gentiles). (That is, the apostles started preaching to the non-Jews, or Gentiles.) If the sin of the Jews (in rejecting Messiah Jesus) brought rich blessings to the rest of the world, think how much greater the blessings will be when the complete number of Jews is included! [Romans 11:11-12] **Most of the believers in the early church during the first century were Jewish; however, the nation of Israel--as a whole--did not receive Him as Messiah.**

Study, and then read again Romans 11:16-24 very carefully. God describes Israel as a cultivated olive tree and the Gentiles (non-Jews) as a wild olive tree. Why should Gentiles NOT despise the Jews? [See verse 18]

_____

_____

_____

What secret truth does the book of Romans teach which will keep the Gentiles from thinking how wise they are? [Romans 11:25]

_____

_____

_____

After the complete number of Gentiles comes to God, then the complete number of Jews will be included. All Israel (those who believe) will be saved. When the Messiah Jesus comes back to Israel, what will he take away from the descendants of Jacob (the Jews)? [Romans 11:26-27]

_____

Because of God's many mercies to us (both Jews and Gentiles), what should we do? [Romans 12:1]

_____

_____

Your next study (Lesson 8 - Part A) will be: *How to Know the News in Advance (Part A).*

How to know the news in advance!

Have you ever wondered what it would be like if you could know the news in advance? You know, not like for a week or two, but for the rest of man's time on earth.

Think how God could use if you had all this information! Well, God has already made it available in "The Revelation" to John (the last book in the New Testament of the Holy Bible). Actually, it is the revelation of Jesus Christ as he made these things known to his servant John. [Revelation 1:1.]

The Bible promises in Revelation 1:3 that you will be blessed if you READ this book (The Revelation), or if you LISTEN to, and OBEY the words of this message of prophecy. It is one of the easiest books in the Holy Bible to outline:

Chapter 1   **The Vision:** What John saw. Instructions to write what would happen in his time ... and in the future.

Chapters 2-3   **Message to the seven churches:** Things which would happen in John's time.

Chapters 4-22   **Future events:** End Time prophetic events.

Read the messages to the seven churches in Chapters 2 and 3. Even though these messages were to churches in Asia Minor (in the area of Turkey) in John's day (about 96-98 A.D.), they have a message to groups of believers in our day - and also to our individual lives.

After you study and answer the questions in both parts of this study (Parts A and B cover Chapters 4 through 22 in the Revelation), **you will know the important world news in advance.**

Chapter 4 shows us a scene in Heaven with 24 elders and four living creatures. The living creatures sings songs of glory and honor and thanks to the one who sits on the throne. What do the elders do as often as the four living creatures give glory to God? [See verses 9-10.]

_____

_____

_____

Chapter 5 shows a scroll in the hand of the one who sits on the throne; but no man in Heaven or earth is found who is worthy to break the seven seals on the scroll and open it. Then there is one who is worthy to open the scroll and look inside - it is the Lion from Judah's tribe who is worthy: the great descendant of David (Jesus, the Messiah of Israel). Why is he found worthy? [Verse 9.]

_____

_____

Chapter 6 describes what happens when the Lamb breaks open the first six of the seven seals. **On a separate page,***** describe what happens when the first six seals are opened. Keep this extra page in a file with your Bible studies (either file it in a hard-copy [paper] file or in one of your computer files … or both).

CAUTION

Do NOT omit this part of the lesson.
You will need this information in the
future days for friends and relatives!!

NOTE: STUDY CAREFULLY & PRAYERFULLY

Seal #1 shows a person who conquers the world without war (he is given a crown). This leader will probably have a lot of military armament (a bow), but does not need to use it (has no arrows).

Seal #2 shows a world war; and Seal #3 a famine.

Seal #4 shows widespread death on the earth. One-fourth of the earth's population is destroyed by the following means:

- War

- Famine

- Disease

- Wild animals

This leaves only 75% of the earth's population. [See Revelation Chapter 6, verse 8.]

Seal #5 shows a scene in Heaven with those who have been martyred (killed) for their faith in Messiah Jesus.

Seal #6 shows great—giant—cosmic disturbances … so severe that people hide themselves in caves and rocks of the mountains afraid because of **the Great Day of God's Wrath that is upon them**.

Chapter 7 describes two different scenes: one on earth, and the other in Heaven. On earth, 144,000 Jewish servants of God are marked in their foreheads (to protect them from harm). In Heaven, there is a crowd so great no one can number the people; they are from every nation, tribe, people, and language.

Who are the people dressed in white robes in Chapter 7? [See verses 13 and 14.]

_____

_____

_____

Chapter 8 starts where Chapter 6 ended. The 7th seal is opened. The 7th seal contains seven trumpets. [See verse 2.] The first four of the seven trumpets are sounded in Chapter 8. In your own words, briefly describe these four trumpet judgments **on a separate page.***** Keep this extra page in a file with your Bible studies (either file it in a hard-copy [paper] file or in one of your computer files).

❈ NOTE ❈

The first four trumpets **were judgments upon natural objects**: the earth, the sea (and ships); the rivers and springs; and the sun, moon, and stars. You can see how they will hurt man's **food supply** (the earth); his **distribution of products** (ships and sea); his **water supply** (rivers and springs); and his **work, or production** (loss of light by which to travel or work).

There are three trumpets left to sound which are known as three horrors or "woes". Chapter 9 describes the first horror (Trumpet #5) and the second horror (Trumpet #6). Describe what these two judgments are like on **a separate page.***** Keep this extra page in a file with your Bible studies (either file it in a hard-copy [paper] file or in one of your computer files).

NOTE "A": Unlike the first four trumpets, where judgment is directed against natural objects, **the 5th and 6th trumpet judgments are against men.**

NOTE "B": Only one-half of the earth's population will be left at this time. One-fourth of the population is destroyed in Revelation 6:8, the 4th seal. This leaves three-fourths, or 75%, one-third of which is destroyed in Revelation 9:18.

NOTE "C": People still do NOT repent of their murders, magic, immorality, or stealing. (Revelation 9:21.) **Magic in this verse includes drugs (or, narcotics), sometimes accompanied by witchcraft.** We know this because of the original Greek word used for magic (or,sorcery): "**pharmakeia**."

Chapter 10 tells of an angel, with one foot on the land and one on the sea, who announces there will be no more delay. When the 7th trumpet sounds, God will begin to accomplish his secret plan.

Chapter 11 tells of **two witnesses who are street preachers**. They proclaim God's message for 3½ years. After they finish their message, the beast out of the bottomless pit (Satan) is allowed to kill them.

What will the people of earth do when the two street preachers are killed? [See Revelation 11:10.]

_____

After 3½ days, a life-giving breath from God enters the dead preachers and they stand up. What happens then? [Read about this in Revelation 11:11-12.]

_____

_____

_____

Then there is another earthquake (the third, so far), and a tenth of the city is destroyed (7,000 people are killed). How do we know that this city where the street preachers are preaching is Jerusalem? [See verse 8.]

_____

This is the end of the second horror, or woe. Then the 7th angel sounds his trumpet (start of the third horror) and announces that the power to rule over the world belongs to our Lord and to his Messiah--the Messiah of Israel--Jesus Christ. Then, another earthquake!

Jesus' Hebrew name is Yeshua HaMashiach

This lesson has been divided into two parts. Your next study (Lesson 8-B) will continue your knowledge of *How to Know the News in Advance (Part B).*

How to know
the news in advance!

In the first half of this study we covered eleven chapters. Remember, we finished Part A after the 7th angel sounded his trumpet [Revelation 11:15.] We will not study what happens as a result of Trumpet #7 being sounded until Chapter 15. The three chapters between [12, 13, and 14] will show us events that will happen meanwhile.

Chapter 12 describes a woman (the nation Israel) who gives birth to a son (Jesus). We know that this woman is Israel by the way she is described in this chapter and also by the description in verse 1. In the Old Testament, Genesis 37:9-11, Joseph had a dream in which his 11 brothers were described as stars. These 12 brothers were the heads of the 12 tribes of Israel. Joseph's parents were the sun and moon in this dream.

The dragon, who is the Devil (see verse 9), stood in front of the woman to devour (eat up) the child as soon as it was born (verse 4). This is how Satan used King Herod when Jesus was born. Herod had all the young male babies, two years and under killed; but Jesus' parents took him to Egypt until Herod died, and so Jesus was safe.

Verse 5 of Chapter 12 tells how Jesus was born and then taken to God and to his throne. These events (the woman who gave birth to a son, and the son going up to God) are NOT future events; they have already happened, as you know. However, they are important events and the Holy Spirit had them recorded in Scripture because they help us to see why Satan hates the Jewish people. Why does Satan hate the Jews? [See Revelation 12:13.]

_____

_____

_____

You see, it was the BLOOD of Jesus on the cross that defeated Satan. The devil hates the people of Israel, because it was through Jewish ancestry (or, family lines) that Jesus was born. There will be a time of great persecution for the Jews in the future. How long will it last? [See verses 6 and 14.]

_____

Chapter 13 describes a beast coming up out of the sea. Who gives him his power? [Re. 13:2.]

_____

People will worship the dragon, who is Satan, and the beast. [See verse 4.] This beast out of the sea is the coming world ruler described here in Chapter 13, verses 5-8, and in other places of the Holy Bible. Who will NOT worship the beast?

_____

_____

This coming world ruler is also known as the "anti-Messiah," the "anti-Christ" and the "false Messiah." He [seemingly] dies and then [it appears as if] his deadly wound is healed.

Another beast is seen coming up out of the earth. [Look at verse 11.] He is the false prophet. He causes people to worship the first beast (the anti-Christ) and to make an image of him. Then, the false prophet (seemingly) gives life to the image of the first beast. **The false prophet**, who **will be the religious head of the world**, forces ALL people to have a mark place on their right hands or in their foreheads. **No one can buy or sell unless they have his mark: the mark is a name, or the number that represents the beast's name.** What is the number of the beast, the mark which people will be forced to take? [Revelation 13:18.]

_____

NOTE: See the last part of the Bonus section at the end of the book, _Frequently Asked Questions_ for more information on the **"Mark of the Beast."**

WARNING

**GOD'S WRATH WILL BE POURED OUT
UPON ALL WHO TAKE THIS MARK.
WARN YOUR FRIENDS AND RELATIVES NOT TO!**

Chapter 14 tells that the great Babylon has fallen who influenced all nations with immoral lust. **All who worship the beast and its image, and receive this mark will be tormented in fire with no relief forever**.

Chapter 15 starts where Chapter 11 ends: at the 7th trumpet. Just for review, remember that there are seven seals. Seal #7 contains seven trumpets; and now we will see that Trumpet #7 contains seven bowls of God's wrath (or, the seven last plagues).

Chapter 16 describes the seven last plagues (the seven bowls of God's wrath). Describe in your own words what each plague is like **on a separate page.***** Keep this extra page of descriptions you write (your answers) in a file with your Bible studies (either file it in a hard-copy [paper] file or in one of your computer files). Describe them briefly like the example below:

Bowl #1   *Painful sores on those who have the mark of the beast and worship his image.* (Example)

CAUTION

**Do NOT omit this part of the lesson.
You will need this information in the
future days for friends and relatives!!**

Chapter 17 describes the great city Babylon as a prostitute. This city causes the leaders and people of the nations to be influenced with immorality. (Re. 17:2.) This great city will be destroyed by the beast, who is the coming world ruler, and by ten kings, or leaders of nations (the 10 horns of Revelation 17:12). These 10 leaders of nations are finally given authority to rule at the same time (one hour, figuratively) with the beast.

What are two ways people will be able to know, or identify, this city in the future? [Verse 6 and verse 18.]

_____

_____

_____

_____

Chapter 18 actually describes the fall announced in Chapter 17. Babylon, the great city, will be hit with plagues in one day and burnt with fire. The businessmen of the earth who trade with her, and who are made rich by that commerce, will be sad because in one hour the city loses everything. Why will the city be punished? [See Revelation 18:23, 24.]

_____

_____

NOTE: In verse 23, we see that the city used magic, or sorcery, to deceive the people of the world. **Magic in this verse includes drugs (or, narcotics), sometimes accompanied by witchcraft.** We know this because of the original Greek word used for magic (or,sorcery): "**pharmakeia**."

Chapter 19 shows the King of Kings and Lord of Lords appearing from Heaven and the armies of Heaven are with him. [Re. 19:14-16.] The kings (or, the leaders) of the earth and their armies gather together to fight against the Lord and his army.

The beast and the false prophet are thrown alive into the lake of fire that burns with sulfur; and the armies of the earth are killed with a sharp sword that comes out of the mouth of the Lord. [Revelation 19:19-20.]

In Chapter 20 we see that Satan is bound for 1,000 years - at the end of the 1,000 years he will be loosed for a little while. Those who were killed for the testimony (or, the truth) of Jesus, and for the Word of God, ... and had not worshipped the beast or his image ... and had NOT taken his mark ... live and rule as kings with Christ for 1,000 years.

After the 1,000 years, Satan is loosed a little while to deceive the nations of the world. The armies of the nations surround the city that God loves (Jerusalem), but fire comes down from Heaven and destroys them.

The devil (Satan) will be cast into the lake of fire and sulfur ... where the beast and false prophet already have been for the 1,000 years during which Satan was bound. How long will they all be tormented? [Read Revelation 20:10.]

Next, is the Great White Throne judgment. Whoever does not have their name in the Book of Life is thrown into the lake of fire. [Read verses 11 through 15 in Revelation Chapter 20.]

Chapter 21 describes a new Heaven and new earth. The holy city, new Jerusalem, comes down out of Heaven.

In Chapter 22, Jesus says, *"Listen, I am coming to you soon*." **Note:** The Greek word here used for "**soon**" is the word "tachu," which can mean "**by surprise**, or suddenly, or quickly."

Your next study (Lesson 9) will be: ***How to Know What's Happening Today!***

LESSON NINE

How to know what's happening today!

In Lesson 7 you learned God's program, or his master plan of the ages. In Lesson 8 you studied some of the important world events that will happen in the future. In this lesson you will find out **what is happening today** - that is, what is really happening!

About two days before Jesus died for our sins on the cross, he told the people of Jerusalem that they would not see him again until they say, "God bless him who comes in the name of the Lord." [Matthew 23:39.]

Jesus left and was going away from the Temple where he had been speaking, when his disciples came to him to show him the Temple's buildings. "Yes," Jesus said, "you may well look at all these. I tell you this: not a single stone here will be left in its place: every one of them will be thrown down."

Later, the disciples came to Jesus in private. [See Matthew 24:1-3.] They asked him three questions:

    1. When will all this be happening?

    2. What will happen to show that it is the time for your coming?

    3. What will happen to show that it is the time for the end of the age?

The disciples were curious. They wanted to know when all this would happen: the Temple being destroyed and Jesus going away until the Jews will say, "God bless him who comes in the name of the Lord."

The Temple was destroyed in the year 70 A.D. by Titus and his Roman soldiers. This was about 40 years after Jesus had warned the people of Jerusalem; and the entire city, as well as the Temple, was destroyed.

But as for the time of the Lord's coming, and of the end of the age, Jesus gave us certain signs to watch for. He answered the disciples questions and told them things that would happen to show when it is time for his coming, and for the end of the age (or, world).

No one knows, however, when that day and hour will come: neither the angels in Heaven, nor the Son (Jesus) ... the Father alone knows. [See Matthew 24:36.]

Whoever, we can know when the time is near, or ready to begin. Read carefully Matthew 24:32-35. How can we know when it is near the time for the Lord to come again to Israel, and for the end of the age, or world? [See verses 33 and 34.)]

_____

_____

_____

Notice what Jesus said in Matthew 24:34. "All these thing will happen before the people now living have all died." In other words, Jesus was saying that the people who are living in the age when these signs start to happen will see all of them come to pass.

Now what are some of these signs that the Lord Jesus mentioned? What did Jesus say will happen to show that it is the time for his return, and for the end of the age? This is what we want to study in the rest of this lesson.

Immediately after the disciples asked Jesus the three questions, Jesus answered, "Watch out, and do not let anyone fool you." Why did he say this? [See Matthew 24:5.]

_____

_____

Jesus said that there would be battles close by and far away (wars and rumors of wars). Why did Jesus say for us NOT to be troubled? [Verse 6.]

_____

56

In Matthew 24:7, what are four (4) signs which are mentioned?

_____

_____

_____

_____

Jesus said that these signs mentioned in verse 7 are like the first pains of childbirth. In other words, the end is not yet: the real pains are yet to come.

Read carefully Matthew 24:9-14. Why will the love of many people grow cold? [Verse 12.]

_____

Where will the Good News about the Kingdom be preached?

_____

_____

What will happen then? [Matthew 24:14.]

_____

Remember what we studied in Lesson 8-A, "*How to Know the News In Advance*?"

Remember the two street preachers who will proclaim God's message for **3½ years**?

Also, remember that there will be a time of great persecution for God's people in the future which will last for **3½ years** [42 months, or 1260 days].!

This 3½ year period is the same period of time that Jesus was talking about in Matthew 24:15-35. The prophet Daniel tells us that a world leader will arrive on the scene who will make a false treaty with the nation of Israel for seven years. But in the middle of the seven years (with 3½ years left), this world leader (who is the anti-Christ) will go into the Temple and stand in the Holy Place pretending as though he is God.

This is what Jesus was talking about when he said, "**The Awful Horror** of which the prophet Daniel spoke, [will be] standing in the holy place." [Matthew 24:15.]

Now, remember the "signs" in verse 7 of Matthew 24 are described as the first pains of childbirth. They tell us that the end is not yet ... BUT NEAR! Jesus will return—soon, quickly—when people are unaware, taking them by surprise. This is why God's Spirit is moving in Israel today; drawing his chosen people, the Jews, back into their land from the four corners of the earth.

This is why we have wars and hear of wars almost daily. Yes, there have always been wars, but there is an increase in world strife today. Since World War II we have had over 50 major conflicts in the world.

This is why we have famine. Famine (shortage of food, and starvation) is on the increase around the world. The increased population rate coupled with the pollution of our natural resources—plus, biowarfare---promises an alarming increase in famine.

This is why we have earthquakes throughout the world. Yes, there have always been earthquakes in history, but the intensity—and frequency---is rising rapidly. Plus, there is an earthquake coming that will be bigger and more destructive than the world has ever known!

All of these signs tell us what is happening today. Jesus will return quickly, when people are unaware, and taking them by surprise!

Your next study (Lesson 10) will be: *How to Let God Use You!*

How to let God use you!

The preacher Paul wrote two letters to the church in the city of Corinth (in Greece). In both letters, Paul appealed to them to be completely united: to work together with only one thought and purpose.

Why did Paul tell the Good News without using the language of man's wisdom? [See 1 Corinthians 1:17.]

_____

_____

1 Corinthians 1:18 tells us: "For the message of Christ's death on the cross is:

_____ to those who are being lost; but for us who are being

saved, it is: _____." < *Write in your answers*

Read 1 Corinthians 1:18-28. Notice that:

- The "**message**" is foolish [verse 18].

- The "**method**" is foolish [verse 21].

- We (the "**messengers**") are foolish [verses 26-28].

NOTICE:

TO BE USED BY GOD IN A MIGHTY WAY ...
YOU HAVE TO BE WILLING TO BE FOOLISH
IN THE EYES OF THE WORLD!

Who then can boast in God's presence? [See 1 Co. 1:29.]

_____

In 1 Corinthians 2:1-2, Paul said that he did not use long words and great learning when he came to preach God's secret truth. Why? [See verse 2.]

_____

Read 1 Corinthians 2:6-9. Notice that there are three kinds of wisdom:

- Worldly wisdom. [verse 6].

- Satanic wisdom, the powers that rule this world. [verses 6, 8].

- God's secret wisdom. [verse 7].

Why cannot the man who does not have God's Spirit (the natural man) receive the gifts that come from God's Spirit? [See 1 Corinthians 2:14.]

_____

_____

What proves that some Christians are still children in the faith, or "men of this world?" [1 Corinthians 3:3.]

_____

What is God's temple? [1 Corinthians 3:16.]

_____

In 1 Corinthians 5:9-13, the Holy Bible says you should not associate with immoral people. This does not mean unbelievers - to avoid them you would have to get out of the world completely! What does it mean? [See verse 11.]

_____

_____

Your body is a part of the body of Christ. Read 1 Corinthians 6:15-20. This is why the Holy Bible warns us to avoid immorality. Every other sin a man commits is without the body; but the man who commits fornication sins against (answer)?

_____

Why should we use our bodies for God's glory? [Vs. 19 & 20.]

_____

_____

_____

Read the command given to married people in 1 Corinthians 7:10-11. A married woman must not leave her husband. What must she do, if she does?

_____

What is one way in which we should be careful towards our brothers (and sisters) in the faith? [1 Corinthians 8:9.]

_____

How should those that preach the Good News get their living? [1 Corinthians 9:1-14.] [See also: Galatians 6:6; Matthew 10:10; 1 Timothy 5:17-18.]

_____

_____

Every temptation that has come your way is the kind that normally comes to people. What will God give you at the time you are tempted? [1 Corinthians 10:13.]

_____

_____

What is God's chain of command? That is, who is supreme (the head) and then next in command, and so on? [1 Co. 11:3.]

_____

_____

_____

_____

Chapters 12, 13, and 14 of 1 Corinthians deal with the gifts of the Holy Spirit, their operation, and worship in the church. It would be well for you to **read these chapters through several times** until you are familiar with them. **List the nine gifts of the Spirit which are mentioned in 1 Corinthians 12:7-11 on a separate page.***** Keep this extra page in a file with your Bible studies (either file it in a hard-copy [paper] file or in one of your computer files).

*** Do NOT omit this part of the lesson. ***
You will need this information to help you be super-productive for God!
And, to access THE BEST God has for you so you can help others.

The Holy Bible says to set your heart on the more important gifts. Best of all, however, is the way of LOVE. Read Chapter 13. Strive for LOVE, and desire spiritual gifts.

Set your heart especially on the gift of [1 Corinthians 13:1] _____
[Write in the answer above.]

Do NOT forbid the _____ *<Write in the answer.*

What is of the greatest importance? [1 Co. 15:3-4.]

_____

Why should you always keep busy in your work for the Lord? [1 Co. 15:58.]

_____

How should we do all our work? [1 Corinthians 16:14.]

_____

_____

Do NOT try to work together as "equals" with those who are unbelievers, for it cannot be done. Why? [Read 2 Corinthians 6:14-18.]

_____

_____

Congratulations! You have just studied through every book in the New Testament. This is **just the beginning of many wonderful experiences** you will have in the Word of God!

Remember to share God's Word with those who do not have it. Many people do not know that God loves them and that He sent his Son, Messiah Jesus, to die for their sins on the cross-stake---and that he is ALIVE---waiting to save them and make them whole!

SPECIAL BONUS

SEE THE NEXT SECTION---*FAQ*---
FREQUENTLY ASKED QUESTIONS

FREQUENTLY ASKED QUESTIONS

● **What are some reasons why people do not receive the Baptism in the Holy Spirit when they pray and ask God for it?**

1. Christ must be Lord [Acts 5:32]
2. Unbelief
3. Wrong motive (proper motive should be to do the work of the Lord … not just for a blessing)
4. Association or participation in or with the occult [Deuteronomy 18:10-12]

● **Why don't we see many of the gifts of the Holy Spirit operating in the churches today?**

In Mark 16:17, Jesus shows us the power that believers have. These signs followed the believers of the early church. The reason why these do not operate completely today is due to the unbelief of modern Christians.

Because you don't speak in tongues does not mean that you are not a born again Christian. It is our faith in Jesus Christ that saves us, not whether we speak in tongues or not.

There is a difference between the "gift" of tongues and "praying in the Spirit". I Corinthians 12:8-11 describes the gifts of the Spirit and Paul includes the gift of tongues which is to be followed by an interpretation of the tongues. This gift is not given to everyone. However, everyone who is baptized in the Holy Spirit receives the manifestation of tongues, which is not followed by an interpretation, but is used to build up each believer. [See 1 Corinthians 14:2.] This is praying in the Spirit. [Also, see 1 Corinthians 14:4.] You see that praying in an unknown tongue edifies the believer, but if we go back to 1 Corinthians 12, we see that the gift of tongues, followed by an interpretation, edifies the church, or the body of believers.

● **Isn't it selfish to want to edify yourself? And how do we know that speaking in tongues isn't just a foreign language we've studied?**

It is NOT selfish to want to build yourself up in the Lord. How can you build up others, or the church, until you're built up? This is why Jude tells us (Jude 20) "But you, beloved, building up yourselves on your most holy faith, praying in the Holy Spirit." The Apostle Paul explains to us in 1 Corinthians 14:14 that "praying in the spirit" is the same as praying in tongues. "For if I pray in an *unknown* tongue, my spirit prays, but my understanding is unfruitful." If Paul were talking about praying in a language he had studied or known -- such as Hebrew, Aramaic, Greek, or Latin -- his understanding would have been FRUITFUL. Remember, Paul said, "I thank my God, I speak with tongues more than all of you." [1 Corinthians 14:18.]

● **Can Satan counterfeit the manifestation of tongues?**

First, let us recommend a book: *The Challenging Counterfeit*, by Raphael Gasson (published by Logos Publishers, Plainfield, NJ 07060). It is written by a Jewish man who was at one time a spiritualist medium, but thanks to God has since been saved, delivered from demons, and baptized in the Holy Spirit. The book shows many ways in which Satan attempts to counterfeit the Holy Spirit and how you can tell the difference.

To answer your question more specifically: If a person asks God in Christ's name for the Holy Spirit, God will NOT give him or her a "false" or demonic tongue. Read Luke 11:5-13 carefully; note particularly verses 11-13. I have personally seen the use of a demonic tongue, but never in a Christian. It was either a case of witchcraft or narcotics; because the person willingly subjected their will to Satan. This is all the more reason that we as God's people should seek the fullness of God's Spirit. We need all the power we can have; thank God for the different gifts of the Spirit!

Remember, you never have a counterfeit unless there is something REAL to copy. In Lesson Eight (a two-part study on the Book of Revelation) of the **Bible Studies**, you will see that the devil even attempts to copy the Holy Trinity. The Baptism in the Holy Spirit, with the initial manifestation of speaking in another language, gives glory to Jesus: it causes a person to LOVE Jesus more, and to hate sin more. It gives the person POWER to do God's work ... along with JOY in the Lord. Only God can do this! Please read 1 Corinthians 12, 13, and 14 again.

● How can a person receive the Baptism in the Holy Spirit?

It is very easy. Remember that it is given to all those who obey God {Acts 5:32]; that God promised to give it to you if you ask Him [Luke 11:13]; and, that the promise is "to as many as the Lord our God shall call" [Acts 2:39].

Don't wait for some feeling to pass over you ... or for God to force anything on you. It's just like being saved. We receive it by FAITH! Just quietly pray to God and ask Him for the Holy Spirit. Expect to receive it! Then, by faith (without waiting on any feeling or any strange sounds), just THANK GOD for baptizing you in the Holy Spirit. As you are thanking Him, simply start praying in another language. It will be your mouth, your tongue doing the praying ... but since you have received the Holy Spirit by faith ... it will be the Spirit praying through you.

Don't worry about what it sounds like; God will understand it. You may think that it is just you, and not the Holy Spirit; but if you have just asked God for the Holy Spirit and have received it by FAITH (regardless of your feelings), then it will be the Holy Spirit helping you to pray. "Likewise, the Spirit also helps our infirmities: for we know not what we should pray for as we ought: but the Spirit himself makes intercession for us with groanings which cannot be uttered." [Romans 8:26]

● Does the initial manifestation of speaking in another language have to accompany the Baptism in the Holy Spirit?

The answer is in the Holy Bible. Read through the five (5) cases outlined in Lesson Four of **Bible Studies**. There are only five cases recorded in the Bible that we may examine (there is another case in Acts Chapter Four, but it was merely a re-filling of those who had been at Pentecost in Acts Chapter Two).

If we examine these five cases objectively, we see that in four of the five, (Acts 2:1-4; Acts 10:46; Acts 19:6; Acts 9:17-18 with 1 Corinthians 14:18). In the fifth case (the case of Simon in Acts Chapter Eight), Simon SAW something that made him KNOW the Spirit had been given to them. It had to be something different than what he had seen before (he had already seen miracles - see Acts 8:13); he probably saw them speak in strange sounds.

For a long time, I taught and believed that one could be filled with the Holy Spirit without the initial manifestation of speaking in other tongues. After receiving this experience, I began to notice that the different gifts of the Spirit began to operate in my life. If one has received the Baptism in the Spirit, the gifts (one or more) as recorded in 1 Corinthians 12, will operate in his or her life.

Many fine Christians have the anointing of the Spirit upon them for witnessing and doing God's work. They recognize from the scriptures that unless the Holy Spirit does the work, they cannot witness or win souls effectively. However, this does not necessarily mean they have received the "Baptism" in the Holy Spirit. This is why they do not experience frequent healings, words of knowledge, etc. -- that is, the gifts of 1 Corinthians 12 do not operate through them.

Many Christians who have NOT received the Baptism in the Spirit will teach that 1 Corinthians 12:13 refers to the Baptism in the Spirit. But if you will examine this passage closely, you will see it is not so. In 1 Corinthians 12:13, the **Holy Spirit is the AGENT**, taking the believer at the instant of salvation and placing the believer into the body of Christ. Now, look at Acts 2:32-33. You will see that in the Baptism in the Spirit, **Jesus is the AGENT**, who pours out the Holy Spirit upon believers. As you will notice in the five examples previously discussed from the Book of Acts, the normal pattern is that believers received the Baptism in the Holy Spirit subsequent to their conversion (except in Acts Chapter 10 where it was simultaneous, as a result of conversion) ... sometimes with the laying on of hands, sometimes without.

● **Can a person be anointed by the Spirit, and still not have the fullness of the Spirit?**

Yes, a person can be anointed by the Spirit, and still not have the "fullness" of the Holy Spirit. Even when one has received the Baptism of the Holy Spirit, it is not the end -- that is, the person has not arrived at some spiritual plateau, or level, in his or her life. The Baptism in the Holy Spirit is just the beginning of a great ministry for Jesus, and it is important that we walk close to Him everyday. Daily ask God to fill you and empower you with His Spirit!

Our daily walk with Jesus is so important! As we walk close to the Lord Jesus, and live by His Word. We will have the increased power in our lives. In Ephesians 5:18, the Holy Bible commands us to be "filled with the Spirit". This is NOT a "one-time" affair, but we are to be filled constantly -- day by day -- second by second. If we sin and grieve the Spirit, the power of God will not be as strong upon us.

"Be ye holy for God is holy." [1 Peter 1:16]

● How does a person sin against, or blaspheme, the Holy Spirit?

"All manner of sin and blasphemy shall be forgiven unto men: but the blasphemy against the Holy Ghost, it shall not be forgiven him, neither in this world, neither in the world to come."

"And whoever speaks a word against the Son of man, it shall be forgiven him, but whoever speaks against the Holy Ghost, it shall not be forgiven him, neither in this world, neither in the world to come." - Jesus [Matthew 12:31-32]

Jesus Christ came to earth to save men; and even if they curse Him and lie about Him, He is willing to forgive them. That's why He died for them: to forgive their sins. However, when a person blasphemes ((speaks evil, abusively, rails, or reviles) against the Holy Spirit, it is another matter. As to Christ's teaching concerning blasphemy against the Holy Spirit (read the context in the case above) ... anyone with the evidence of the Lord's power before their eyes, who should then declare it (that power) to be Satanic, exhibits a condition of heart beyond Divine illumination and, therefore, hopeless! As to the Son of Man, in His humiliation upon earth at His first coming, there might have been misunderstanding, but not so with the Holy Spirit's power demonstrated.

● Is it possible to receive anything else but the Gift of Tongues?

Yes! Ask God for any of the gifts you desire in your heart. It is the Spirit that gives them as he wills, but God told us to desire spiritual gifts, especially that we may prophesy. [1 Corinthians 14:1.] Read Prince Handley's book, *How to Receive God's Power with Gifts of the Spirit*, available at Amazon and other book stores.

All (people) do not have the gift of tongues, but all who have been baptized in the Holy Spirit can speak in tongues. There is a difference in the GIFT of tongues and speaking in tongues. The GIFT of tongues is a special gift given to bring a message to people gathered in church. It is (normally) accompanied by its twin gift, the gift of interpretation, which is the ability to explain to the people in the church what the message in tongues means. It is one way God has of speaking to the church. The Holy Bible says, "Let him that speaks in an unknown tongue pray that he (himself) interpret." [1 Corinthians 14:13.] If he is not able to interpret, then someone else in the church should interpret who has the ability. If there is no interpreter, then he should keep silent. [1 Corinthians 14:27-28.]

As mentioned above, not all (people) have the GIFT of tongues, but all (who have been baptized in the Holy Spirit) can speak in tongues. The GIFT is for a message to the church, but just speaking in tongues (praying in the Spirit) may be done by a person when he or she is simply praying to God. Read 1 Corinthians 14:14: "For if I pray in an unknown tongue, my spirit prays, but my understanding is unfruitful." If you pray in English (or your mother-tongue) you understand; that is, your understanding is fruitful.

But if you pray in a strange language, you don't understand it. But God does! ! Corinthians 14:2 tells us, "For he that speaks in an **unknown tongue** speaks not unto men, but unto God: for no man understands him; howbeit **in the Spirit** he speaks mysteries (secret truths). When you pray in the Spirit (speak in tongues), you are praying to God in secret truths by His Spirit.

There are several reasons for wanting to speak in tongues:

It is a supernatural way of praising God (see Acts 10:43-46).

It is a supernatural and sure way of praying according to the will of God (see Romans 8:26-27).

It is a rest and a refreshing (see Isaiah 28:11-12).

It is a way of edifying (building up) oneself (see I Corinthians 14:4 and Jude verse 20).

As soon as we are saved, we are baptized into the body of Christ by the Holy Spirit (1 Corinthians 12:13). That is, the Holy Spirit places us into the body of Christ, the universal church of all believers. But this is NOT the "Baptism in the Holy Spirit" where Jesus as the BAPTIZER pours out the Spirit upon believers (see Acts 2:33). You are already in the Body of Christ if you know Jesus. Now, ask God for the Baptism in the Holy Spirit so you will have the POWER to serve Him!

● **I have asked God to baptize me in the Holy Spirit ... I did not receive the language. Why?**

Sometimes there is a misunderstanding as to what speaking in tongues really is. The Holy Bible says, "For if I pray in an unknown tongue, my spirit prays, but my understanding is unfruitful." In other words, you ... or your mind ... won't understand it. So don't worry about what it sounds like, or whether you can understand it. Just release your tongue in faith and speak as the Holy Spirit guides you.

See Acts 2:4: "And **THEY** ... began to speak with other tongues, as the Spirit gave them utterance." **YOU** do the speaking -- use your mouth, your tongue, your throat -- and because you have prayed to God in FAITH, confessing Jesus as your Lord, you know that what you speak will be from God ... but **YOU** do the speaking! As you praise God in your new language, you will be speaking secret truths by the power of the Spirit [1Corinthians 14:2]. Luke 11:13 tells us " ... how much more shall your heavenly Father give the Holy Spirit to them that ask him?" If you ask God in FAITH for the Baptism in the Holy Spirit, he is NOT going to give you a false or demon tongue!! Read the next section below.

● **Concerning 1 Corinthians 14:22, aren't tongues just for a "sign" to unbelievers?**

That's just ONE of the purposes for tongues, as mentioned earlier.

There are many people today who have received Christ as a result of hearing a Christian speak in their heavenly language (tongues), when the speaker did NOT know the language he was speaking. I personally know a wonderful brother (who was a millionaire for over 35 years), a medical doctor and an engineer, who heard a brother in Christ that I know speak in Arabic. My friend did NOT know Arabic. This doctor became a mighty servant of God!

There are thousands of people today who are receiving the Bible experience of the Baptism in the Holy Spirit. **It is for us today!** Acts 2:39 says: **"For the promise (see verse 33) is unto you, and to your children, and to <u>all</u> that are afar off, even as many as the Lord our God shall call."** There is a great revival in the world, and it is growing every day. God is pouring out His Spirit and the GIFTS of the Holy Spirit are operating in and through many Christians. Many unbelieving Christians try to teach that the GIFTS of the Spirit were just a "crutch" to help the early church get started. The idiocy of that argument is obvious by observation and by history: If the early church needed a crutch with all the miracles performed and people saved … how much more does the church today need the GIFTS?!

● When I pray in tongues it sounds "strange" to me. Why?

That's what the Bible says: "otra linguas" … other tongues … strange languages! At a place where I ministered frequently a Philippino man kept saying one word over and over. He thought God didn't want to baptize him in the Spirit. However, what he was saying was a word for "Lord" in a language an Egyptian friend of mine spoke. He kept repeating "Lord, Lord, Lord!"

Sometimes this happens when a person receives the Baptism in the Holy Spirit. Just pray and thank God for the Holy Spirit. Then continue to pray and praise God with these new sounds … your NEW language. You will probably begin to experience a fuller release of a distinct, but different language. When I received the Baptism in the Spirit, it was like a flock of heavenly doves flying out of my mouth. I spoke in tongues off and on for hours. It has now been almost 30 years and I still can't praise Him enough in my new language. What a merciful God … I used to teach people NOT to seek the Baptism in the Spirit. God forgive me!!!

I recommend you study my book, *How to Receive God's Power with Gifts of the Spirit*, available in both e-Book and Paperback at Amazon and other stores.

● **I think there is too much emphasis on speaking in tongues.**

Thank you for your honest comments. You will see that we agree with you in Lesson Ten of the **Bible Studies**. The Holy Bible says to set your heart on the more important gifts. Best of all, however, is the way of LOVE [1 Corinthians 13]. Strive for love and desire spiritual gifts. Set your heart especially on the gift of speaking God's messages ... but do NOT forbid the speaking with strange sounds. See 1 Corinthians 14:1 and 39.]

● **Does it say anywhere in the Bible that coffee and tea are stimulants and that you shouldn't drink them?**

Nowhere in the Holy Bible does it say that coffee and tea are bad. I do not drink coffee, but just because I don't drink coffee doesn't mean that somebody else should not. Always ask God to show you what he would have you to do, and not to do. [See James 1:5]

● **It's wrong for me to judge others. What am I supposed to say when I'm asked to give an opinion of someone?**

When you're asked to give an opinion of someone, always look for something good in their life about which you can share. Try to lift people up, and not to tear them down. However, there may be times when you may have to give an objective appraisal of someone. In that case, do what the Bible says. In Matthew 7:1 we are instructed by Jesus, "Judge not, that you be not judged." Never judge a person's inward motives ... that is, the reason for which they do certain things. However, in the same chapter (Matthew 7), Jesus tells us, "A good tree cannot bring forth evil fruit ... you shall know them by their fruits." [Matthew 7:16-20] You can know a person by what they do outwardly ... or by what issues forth from their life. Finally, judge production ... not motives.

● How can I witness for Christ?

There are many ways. You can call people on the telephone -- just go through the phone book and pick out names. Call them and tell them about Jesus. You can write people letters. You can take your Bible to the nearest shopping center, or street corner, and start talking to people or preaching about Jesus. Give your testimony ... you know what God has done for you! And If you only know one verse of scripture, like John 3:16, you have all the information you need to get started! If you don't feel the liberty to preach, then you can always hand out some Gospel literature. You may want to buy or bake a cake or pie and take it to your neighbor, a sick person, a homeless person, or a rich person ... and tell them about Jesus!

Whenever you go to talk to someone about Jesus, **always pray first and ask the Holy Spirit to prepare their heart**. Ask God to fill you with his Spirit and give you the words to speak. Remember to tell them that God loves them and He sent Christ to die for their sins on the cross. Tell them Jesus is alive and will save them NOW if they ask Him! Sometimes you will be able to pray with the person right there and lead them to Christ. You can lead them in a short prayer and have them ask Christ to forgive their sins and save them.

● What is the real importance of prayer; why do people talk about "spending time with God"?

Concerning prayer, time spent with God is very important. The more we seek God in prayer, the more of his nature, grace, and power will he endow to us. However, just the fact that we say we take time to be with God, doesn't mean we are seeking him. Sometimes it may be more advantageous to just sit (or stand) and talk to him ... and then listen to him talk back. It may take some time -- maybe a few minutes, maybe a few hours -- for us to really wait on him to be able to communicate. Other times, it may be more to our advantage to really get down to business and PRAY for only a few minutes. But the important thing is that we start every day alone with God in prayer ... and end the day in the same manner.

Throughout the day, pray without ceasing by mentally praising God, seeking his face for wisdom, talking to him ... all of this interspersed with praying in tongues. If you do not pray in tongues during these times, there will be:

No opportunity for the Holy Spirit to override your prayers (in case they are wrongly directed or have error in motivation);

No opportunity for the Holy Spirit to initiate prayers of his own through you--- which YOU might not or would not do.

Finally, ask God to make you a person of prayer, fasting, and his Word. He **will** because you will be praying according to God's will. Fasting will keep the anointing fresh in your life. If for no other reason ... do these things for other people who God wants to reach through you. "The world is the field."

● Why do I need to keep on praying for some things even though I believe I have it?

Read and study Lesson Two: How To Talk To God in the Bible Studies. There are some things we pray for which require persistent prayer. Not all things ... but some things. One reason may be that we have not truly prayed in the manner prescribed in one of the first five doors (see Lesson Two). For example, maybe we have not really believed by faith that we have received it already (Door 5), and so we need to keep praying until God answers.

Another reason may be that it just happens to be something for which God wants us to keep on asking. Maybe God wants to see how sincere we really are. This is where many people give up. Think of some examples of when you were a child; how there were some things you wanted for which you had to keep asking. Look up the following cases in your Bible where people prayed to God persistently:

Genesis 32:26 - 1 Samuel 15:11 - Esther 4:16 - Matthew 15:21-28 - Luke 6:12 - James 5:17 - 1 Kings 17:19-22 - 1 Kings 18:42-44.

"And he (Jesus) spoke a parable unto them to this end, that men ought always to pray, and not to faint." [Luke 18:1-8]

● How can I be free "forever" from condemnation feelings around certain people?

First of all, man was created in the image of God. Adam sinned and your fellowship had to be restored to God through the shed blood of his son, Jesus Christ. Now that you are restored, you are no longer under condemnation.

"There is therefore now no condemnation to them which are in Christ Jesus ..." [Romans 8:1]

You're somebody! You are very important!! To God, to yourself ... and to others to whom God has assigned you!!! Ephesians 1:4 tells us, "Long ago, even before he made the world, God chose us to be his very own through Christ; (he decided then) that we should be holy and without fault (standing) before him (covered) in love."

If God says you don't have a fault (the word "fault" here means "blemish"), and if you are COVERED with his love, then you can learn to love yourself ... in spite of what someone else thinks about you; even in spite of what you think about yourself!

Since you are FREE, and since God enjoys you, why not enjoy yourself?

⬤ Why does the Bible sometimes talk about the bad things people have done?

The Holy Bible is a very honest book. If people had written the Bible, instead of God, it would probably tell all the nice things about men and women. (See Jeremiah 17:9 and Romans 3:23.) The Bible tells it as it is; but thank God it also gives us an answer. The only answer to our problems: Jesus Christ.

⬤ Why does God allow Satan to stand before him and accuse the brethren?

There's a lot of things about God that we don't know; but everything we need to know is revealed in the Word of God. Why God allows Satan to be an accuser of the brethren, we don't really know [Revelation 12:10]. But what we do know is that Satan's nature is: deception, pride, accusation, theft, murder, destruction, fear, and hate! Just the OPPOSITE of Jesus! It doesn't matter how much Satan tries to accuse you, or any Christian, because the shed BLOOD OF CHRIST has not only defeated Satan, but it has CLEANSED and LOOSED you from your sins!

The devil is the most frustrated being in the universe today. He runs "to and fro seeking to devour whom he may" [1 Peter 5:8]. He knows his time is running out, for the Bible says " ... and the devil that deceived them was cast into the lake of fire and brimstone, where the beast and the false prophet are, and shall be tormented day and night forever and ever." [Revelation 20:10] Satan can never do anything unless God allows him to. Everything the devil does, or has done, fits into God's plan. God can turn around even the bad if you will release the situation(s) to Him in faith. Faith and forgiveness are "twins" that will turn around any situation!

Make sure that you don't accuse God's people, the brethren. For then, you would be doing something that God won't allow the devil to do: and that is going beyond the BLOOD OF JESUS! One of the names for the devil actually means "slanderer". We should never slander another Christian ... or anyone, for that matter! To slander another Christian---even if what we are saying is true---is to do something that God won't even let the devil do. Satan may accuse you---and the brethren---but it is to no avail, because Jesus is defending you at the Father's right side. He is your attorney, as well as your judge. Remember, your Judge is your Righteousness [2 Corinthians 5:21]. You have a PERFECT Savior ... and a PERFECT salvation! Satan and his accusations can NOT pass beyond the BLOOD OF CHRIST!

Note: For a full description of Job's trials and victory (after Satan accused him before God), study the book, *Health and Healing Complete Guide to Wholeness*, available at Amazon and other book stores. (It is in both e-Book and print formats.)

● **I am a corrupt person, and I think I am predestined to go to hell. Also, I cheat a lot. Can you help me?**

Thanks for writing me. Please excuse me for taking so long to answer. I've been away serving God but have been praying for you. Today I preached in a large high school and several were saved. When you said in your mail that you are a corrupt person, it made me think of what the Word of God says: "There is none righteous, no not one." [Romans 3:10] God says we are all corrupt, and that is why he sent Jesus to die for my sins and your sins on the cross [see Romans 5:8].

Even though you don't go to any Bible studies or church, you can still read and study God's Holy Word by yourself. Anytime you need help or want to talk, contact our E-mail mentorhelp@gmail.com. Either I, or someone who loves the Lord, will be happy to talk and pray with you.

You do not have to worry about being predestined to go to hell, because the Holy Bible says: **"The Lord is ... NOT willing that any should perish, but that all should come to repentance."** [2 Peter 3:9] If you really want to be saved, God will save you! Just believe what he has told you in his Word. John 1:12 says, **"But as many as received him, to them gave he power to become the sons of God, even to them that believe on his name."**

God has never sent anyone to hell. If a person dies and goes to hell, it is because that person refused to receive Christ as their savior. God sent Christ so that we could be saved if we want to. "Whosoever will may come."

● **I don't understand about "predestination" and "freewill"; don't they contradict each other?**

The Holy Bible shows that man has a free will. There are many verses which tell us this. For example, Romans 10:13: "Whosoever shall call upon the name of the Lord shall be saved." Whosoever will, may come! But the scriptures also show that whoever comes to Christ and receives him has been elected (or, predestined) by God. The Bible tells us in John 6:44, "No man can come to me (said Jesus), except the Father which has sent me draw him: and I will raise him up at the last day." It is God who draws us by the power of his Holy Spirit to trust in the Lord Jesus Christ.

For centuries men have tried to explain how man could still have a free will if it is God who draws him (that is, if God is the one who determines his election). But don't let this bother you. We can never figure out God's ways. The Bible says in Isaiah 55:8-9, "For my thoughts are not your thoughts, neither are your ways my ways, says the Lord ... so are my ways higher than yours." Someday when we get to Heaven, maybe the Lord will explain to us this great mystery. But for now, we can be thankful that the Lord has brought us to himself.

77

To man, truth has to be one way or the other. That is, man likes to have an answer in one category or another: like "freewill" or "destination". But to God, some truths may be "parallel" ... He is the TRUTH! One thing we know is that God didn't want us to be robots; otherwise he would have made us that way! He wants people who love him and worship, serve, and praise him of their own volition. Anyone who wants to be saved can be saved.

God gave you a FREE WILL. One day you exercised this free will and decided to give your life to Christ. Even though you exercised this free will which God has given you---there was a time when God looked FORWARD (even before he framed the world into existence)---and he saw (ahead of time) that you would make a decision to let Christ be your Lord. So even though God gave you a free will, you were ELECTED before the world began! God loves you and want the BEST for you!

● **I hear people, and Bible teachers, say that the Jewish temple must be rebuilt. Why?**

Read 2 Thessalonians 2:4. The "man of sin" (the "anti-Christ", or "false Messiah") will go sit in the temple, showing himself as though he is God. Therefore, the temple MUST be rebuilt in the future.

God's prophetic time clock runs in relation to Israel. Notice that in Daniel 9:24-27 there are two main time periods mentioned. One is a period of 69 weeks (Hebrew "heptad", or weeks of 7 years each), and the second is a period on one week, which is the 70th week (seven years). The 69 weeks ended when Christ died on the cross (see Daniel 9:26).

The Messiah was "cut off" but not for himself; and God's prophetic time-clock stopped. It will NOT start again until the start of the 70th week, or the period of time known as the seven year tribulation. The last half of the seven years ... the last 3.5 years ... is that period of time known as the great tribulation: the time of "Jacob's trouble" [Jeremiah 30:7]. It is in the middle of this 70th week that the anti-Christ goes into the rebuilt temple [see Daniel 9:27, Matthew 24:15, 2 Thessalonians 2:4]. This last 3.5 years of the 70th week Daniel talked about will be a time of worse persecution for Israel and the Jews than they have ever known: exceedingly more terrible than Nazi Germany! Many Jews will turn to the Messiah during this time.

For a detailed study of the Jews and the end-times, including signs of the times, and future events, study again Lessons 7, 8A, 8B and 9.

● Does the rapture of the church start God's time-clock "ticking" again?

There are different views among scholars as to when the rapture is. Some feel it is before---at the start---of the seven year tribulation. Some feel it is at the middle of the seven years. And some feel it is at the end of the seven year tribulation. These are known as the "pre", "mid", and "post" tribulation rapture theories. I started studying all of these views in depth, not only in graduate schools of theology, but also on my own, over 50 years ago. The "catching away" ("harpazo" in Greek) or gathering of the saints in the air to meet Christ when he returns is a scriptural fact as declared in 1 Thessalonians 4:14-18.

It seems that God's prophetic time-clock will start at the beginning of the seven year tribulation. The important thing is to be ready---to be looking for and loving the return of Christ to earth (His 2nd coming)---no matter **what** happens or **when** it happens. Don't ever let whatever view you hold, or feel is correct, ("pre", "mid", or "post) keep you from fellowship with other Christians who may hold another view. The basis of all fellowship is the fact that Jesus bought us with his BLOOD!

● When the Bible talks about days, does it mean literal days?

Wherever possible, and where the context gives evidence, take the time mentioned as a literal unit of time. That is, when the Bible mentions a year, it usually means a year. When it mentions a day, it usually means a day. There are certain construction of grammar, especially in Hebrew, which sometimes show us that it should be other than literal. This happens to be the case in Daniel Chapter Nine. In Genesis Chapter One, however, it seems the days are literal 24 hour days (evening and the morning); when the Hebrew word for day ["yom"] is connected with a number (as in "and the evening and the morning were the third day"), it usually has reference to a literal 24 hour day.

● I don't understand what the "transgression of desolation" is in Daniel Chapter Eight.

It is interesting to compare Daniel Chapter Eight with secular history. There has already been a "transgression of desolation" in the Jewish temple; however, it was just a "type" (an actual happening that symbolized another future similar happening ... a symbol of a future occurrence). If you will notice Daniel 8:1-12 describes: 1) a ram with two horns; and, 2) a he-goat. Also, verses 15-27 give the interpretation of the same, which was a vision that appeared to Daniel. Notice in verse 20, the ram with the two horns represented the two kings of Media and Persia (this empire lasted from 536 BC to 333 BC). In Daniel 8:21, the he-goat was the King of Greece (Alexander the Great, who conquered that part of the civilized world in 333 BC).

Notice in this vision which Daniel had, verse 8 tells that the he-goat had a great horn on his head which was broken, and then four (4) other notable horns came up. The interpretation in verse 22 tells us that these were four kingdoms which stood up (arose) out of that nation (the Grecian empire). These were: Syria, Egypt, Macedonia, and Asia Minor. Now notice verse 9 says that out of one of the four notable horns cane forth a little horn. Verse 11 tells that the little horn took away the daily sacrifice out of the sanctuary ... and there was a transgression of desolation following.

● Who, or what, was the "little horn" mentioned in Daniel 8:9?

This "little horn" was Antiochus Epiphanes who was the king of Syria. He, the "little horn", was a type (or, picture) of the "other" horn [out of the ten horns] spoken of in Daniel 7:20-25, the SAME as the anti-Christ (or, anti-Messiah) of Revelation Chapters 13 and 17. Now I will give you some historical facts to show you what Antiochus did when he came into Jerusalem about 170 B.C.

1. He sacrificed a sow (female pig) upon the alter of burnt offerings; and then made a broth from it and sprinkled it over the entire building.
2. He corrupted the young people with lewd practices and obscenity.
3. He changed the Feast of Tabernacles to the feast of Bacchus.
4. He auctioned off the priesthood.
5. All true worship was forbidden.
6. Idol worship was introduced (especially to Jupiter Olympus).
7. The city was devastated; 100,000 Jews were massacred.

Notice that Antiochus was a type or picture of that man of sin who will appear in the future and shall magnify himself against the Prince of princes, Messiah Jesus, (see Daniel 8:25); notice that he (the man of sin) will be "broken without hand." I Have gone into detail on this to show you how some prophecies have a partial, or even complete fulfillment; but the initial fulfillment is just a type of that which is to come. You can usually tell this in these types of prophetic passages by the clear wording applied to the portion yet to be fulfilled.

Remember, that in Daniel 9:27 **the anti-Christ (the false-Messiah) shall confirm a covenant with the children of Israel for seven years**. Also, the ten horns in Daniel 7 and in Revelation 13 and 17 show a ten nation confederacy in the end time. The nations, along with Russia, Ethiopia, Libya, and Persia (Persia being the partial confines of modern day Iran) coming against Israel are the things to watch for right now.

● **If a person really wants to commit sin (inside themselves) ... I bet they still commit the sin.**

Yes, if a person really desires to sin, they probably will; however; a person who loves the Lord Jesus and wants to serve him can successfully can resist Satan no matter how great the temptation. **James 4:7 says, "Resist the devil and he will flee from you."** Notice the first condition is, **"Submit yourself to God."**

In James 5:14-15, the "elders" are the seasoned leaders of the church, or local place of worship. In the early Christian church such designations as elder, presbyter and bishop, if not strictly synonymous, were interchangeable (Acts 20:17; Titus 1:5-7). Elders cooperate with the apostles in the government of the church (Acts 15 verses 2, 4, 6, and 22, and Acts16:22). They had the spiritual care of the congregation. You can see this in 1 Timothy 3:5, 5:17; Titus 1:9; and 1 Peter 5:1-4.

I think you really want to know: Why are we to live holy? We are to live holy because our Father in Heaven is holy! Holiness is his very nature, and if we have been saved and are God's children, then we, also, should have the nature of God in us. We should also want to live holy to PLEASE God. In Romans 12:1, the Apostle Paul said, " I beseech *(or plead with)* you, brothers, by the mercies of God, that you present your bodies a living sacrifice, holy, acceptable unto God, which is your reasonable service."

81

To PRESENT your body means that you give God a PRESENT; that is, a presentation ... a GIFT, if you will. And Paul is saying here, "I beg you to **give God a present: your body** as a holy sacrifice which he can accept; **seeing that God has been so merciful to you, by granting you salvation that you didn't deserve.** He gave the BEST He had---his only Son, who died a cruel death for you, to pay for your sins---now give your BEST to Him! Show God you're thankful, and give Him your body, HOLY, so that he may accept it." If we are NOT God's children, but still belong to Satan, then we will not have a desire to live holy. This is one way we can check to make sure we are saved!

⬤ **Can you explain more about the "Mark" of the Beast? I have heard it may refer to Islam.**

Yes, there is another view concerning the "666" in the Brit Chadashah (New Testament) being a numerical equivalent to the name of the "False Messiah" (or, the anti-Christ).

REASON: In Yochanan's (John's) day---when he received the Revelation from Mashiach Yeshua---he wrote "<u>what he SAW</u>."

NOTICE: He could have seen Arabic (the 666) written from "right to left" instead of Greek. Also, the Greek word for "number" is "arithmos" and could mean "multitude." Therefore, if he SAW Arabic (instead of Greek "666"), the whole meaning of the passage in Revelation 13:18 would change to: *" ... the multitude in the name of allah."*

WHY? Because one of the Arabic characters could be "X" showing two crossed swords instead of the Greek letters (the 22nd, 14th, and an obsolete letter as a cross). Islamic warriors wear the armband of "allah" on their forehead and on their right arm when they go to war "in the name of allah."

QUESTION: Did the Ruach Elohim (the Spirit of God) show ahead of time the growth and evil world goals of Islam 500 years before it originated through the satanic inspiration of Muhammad?

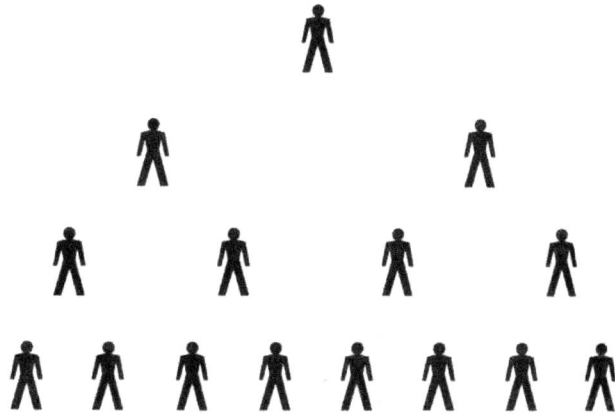

Now ... YOU go teach other people!

LIVE A LIFE OF EXCELLENCE!

UNIVERSITY OF EXCELLENCE PRESS
Los Angeles ■ London ■ Tel Aviv

OTHER BOOKS BY PRINCE HANDLEY

- Map of the End Times

- How to Do Great Works

- Flow Chart of Revelation

- Action Keys for Success

- Health and Healing Complete Guide to Wholeness

- Prophetic Calendar for Israel and the Nations (2014-23)

- Healing Deliverance

- How to Receive God's Power with Gifts of the Spirit

- Healing for Mental and Physical Abuse

- Victory Over Opposition and Resistance

- Healing of Emotional Wounds

- How to Be Healed and Live in Divine Health

- Healing from Fear, Shame and Anger

- How to Receive Healing and Bring Healing to Others

- New Global Strategy: Enabling Missions

- The Art of Christian Warfare

- Success Cycles and Secrets

AVAILABLE AT AMAZON AND OTHER BOOK STORES
UNIVERSITY OF EXCELLENCE PRESS

www.ingramcontent.com/pod-product-compliance
Lightning Source LLC
Chambersburg PA
CBHW080525030426
42337CB00023B/4636